Resume Writing 2015

Up to date resume writing guide to get you hired in 2015

Table of Contents

Introduction – A Personal Branding Document!

Want to hitch yourself to a fly jet to land on to a job of your dreams? Want success desperately but do not know where to start? However, give yourself a reminder that success does not occur overnight – it is a series of consistent efforts made over the years.

Having said this, you need to understand that your previous performance will have a deep impact as to how you are treated in the world of jobs. However, if you have the ability, vigor and passion to succeed, your skills can surely get you to it! Note that when it comes to professional life, it is your professional skills rather than education, which count the most. Nothing to worry about! You just need some right insight regarding the issue and your journey towards success will begin now.

Take the first step towards success by finding a job. Yes, getting employed is the desire and for this, you need to start searching for jobs. You can surely find a job, but what ensures that you are taken up for it is the 'resume'.

A resume is nothing less than a personal branding document. This implies that your personal branding document needs to be well-equipped with the right, high-quality information which includes an excellent personal branding statement. This personal branding will actually allow you to communicate yourself in the professional world.

A resume ranks amongst those documents that pertain to be highly important in a professional career. It is that valuable piece of paper, which not only addresses what have you accomplished in the past, but what the future holds for you! It therefore entails that a resume will determine whether you are getting the call for job interview or whether you are going to stay at home!

A meaningful and high-quality resume is evocative of your skills, enables the employers to distinguish you amongst numerous other participants as well as allows them to know what makes you so special that you stand out from others.

As a resume allows an insight into your life, abilities and knowledge, you must ensure that it is up to the mark. This is crucially important because having applied for a job, you do not actually get to physically talk to the company. All you can do is send your resume, which will speak itself. And because you are not there to undo any mistakes by the use of buttering language or covering it all up, it needs to be ensured that your resume seems highly professional and greatly competitive. Note that a mass of people are going to apply for the job you are applying for, so what is it that will help ease the company sort out you amongst the selected candidates? Yes, you are right In guessing – it is your resume!

A resume basically communicates why are you different, what makes you capable, why are you deserving and which of your professional skills can help the company attain success? A resume delivers the first impression about you, therefore you must try to be very concerned about it! It thus entails that you create a lasting impression which creates memory and enables you to reach a position which is reminiscent of success.

Bear in mind that the employers will have hundreds of resumes to go through and this process will surely make them overwhelmed. In order to make an impact upon them with just one document seems like a tough job. But knowing what makes up a good resume and a bad resume can enable you to find a job of your dreams!

Resume Writing Tips - Things to do!

Keeping in mind that the resume reveals everything about you, you should try to ensure that the resume is counted amongst the good ones. There are a few dos that will help you cope up with the changing standards and make your resume appear more interesting, appealing and worth considering. Though the debate for what is considered a good resume continues, it is worth assuring that your resume is not lengthy enough but is filled with quality information.

The prime trend for 2015 you must focus on is brevity. As the trends evolve and time gets to be valued, employers tend to value content that is concise and to the point. This concept is becoming increasingly popular and calls for targeted positioning. As resume is a self-branding document, messages and content, which can effectively market you in brief statements are a must.

Once you know how you need to approach your self-branding document, easy to follow points are evocative of a good resume. The points must be presented in a flow and must be simple for the employer to understand. This proves the point that short branding statements are taking place of the traditional lengthy profiles, which once used to be a salient feature of the resume.

Thirdly, emphasize on your working experience, especially the most recent jobs. This is important because the prime focus of employers is the most recent job role that you are either serving or were serving prior to your job application. This is because you are likely to be well versed with the tasks and skills you used on your last role and therefore, that can do your prospective employer much good. Based upon your last role, your new employer may choose to train or develop you further in that discipline. This can be mutually beneficial to both of you.

Fourthly, you must be versatile enough to put different experiences in accordance with the job requirements. As the trends evolve and diversity is what is required from the prospective employees, multiple-part time roles and short-term contracts must be vividly presented in your resume. The essence is presenting to your employer a diversified experience and versatility that can make you respectable in the eyes of the employer.

Fifthly, ensure that your personal branding document is a mix of right keywords. As employers have been seeing resumes that are too stuffed up with the keywords, it is crucial that you use keywords that are specific to you and make your resume appear more personal. Thus, it will not look like a template but rather your very personal document. Having an emphasis on the right keywords, which are well-integrated in the resume increase the probability of your resume being read and therefore, the chance of you getting selected. Be cautious of adding extra keywords – only related and supported words are worthy of being added in your resume. All other words must be considered extra and therefore, avoided.

Next, you should be aware that 2015 is the year of design. You must be wary of the format and design of your resume as much as you are wary of your image. Using savvy designs and formats as part of the document will enable you to attract the employer to take a glance at your resume and might also be a source of temptation for the employer to read further. The design will simply portray your delicacy and compactness to the employer, which can be a major difference in you getting the job or staying back at home.

Next to design comes the color. Modern resumes tend to have colorful hints, headers for parting out different sections as well as different types of decorative lines, images, attractive fonts and boxed wording in order to captivate the attention of the employer.

Lastly, commit to your memory that resumes are nothing but a document that tells your career story. Therefore, they must be different from career obituaries. You must learn to focus on value and avoid anything that is boring like generic tasks or interviews. Instead, tell what you have achieved, how you have achieved and how you want to further accomplish things in your career. This is the underpinning point of your success and will bring you the right job!

Things to consider

Your resume must be a snapshot of your personal and work history. The branding document must provide for the attributes that are evocative of success. It therefore entails that you have provided details of past accomplishments as well as how you are beneficial for the employer.

The main thing that will have a lasting impact will be the branding statement. Therefore, there are some important aspects to consider when creating your branding statement.

You first need to consider how you appear to the outer world. It is a fact that your outlook and aptitude has guided you to find your way into the field you are now in and enabled you to develop the required talents. It proves that your stance on life has a deep impact onto how you create your personal statement. What is required is that you need to give some serious consideration to your long term vision. This should include how you intend to impact the people around you. Whether you want them to correspond in a better manner? Whether you want to expand the already existing technology being used in a company? Think about ways that can help you brand yourself in a manner that ensures that you are of ample benefit to the employers and deliver these specifications in your statement.

Next, focus on your goals. It is important for an employer to know that the prospective employees have a keen focus and are committed to get the goals accomplished. You must therefore deliver that you have been achieving goals in the past and intend to do so in the future. Thus, career goals are of immense importance when creating a personal branding statement. This will mean how you want to bring about the difference. Begin by writing what you want to achieve and link them to your skills that will enable you to attain your goals.

Lastly, give thorough consideration to your attributes what can also be called as brand attributes. Having recognized them, you need to apply them to your personal and professional history in the light of the current job requirements. An idea that can help you sprout up as a good professional is to have a set of words, at least three, that are descriptive of your professional attributes. Leader, developer, thinker, visionary, innovator, modernizer or manager– what are those three words that perfectly suit you?

The Approach

You need to plan your career before making any resume. Once you have determined the course of action, you can go on to discover your skills and interests that are to form part of your resume.

When making up your resume to match the current trends, you need to come up with something that is attractive, concise and striking for the employer. As the resumes compete to find their way, making you amongst the qualified candidates, having them altered as per the needs of the time and up-to-date information can undoubtedly make a difference.

- **Deliver your image by using the right words**

You might be tempted to include the wrong words in your resume. This is because you are not properly guided to move into the right direction or you might not simply know that such words are not needed. As mentioned, avoid key words that are not contextual. For example, including phrases like "I am a passionate individual" or "trying to focus on the ultimate goals, I am driven by the energy" without anything to back them up might cause you damage. This is because such phrases make your resume complicated, and through your resume you are basically delivering your image. Being passionate while delivering the work can be evident from your actions, and relating it to such actions can help.

For instance, you can tell how you felt about a specific job by focusing on how you achieved certain things – the profitability and improved performance. Or you can show how you helped other team members regardless of the opposition faced. These better describe your role.

> **Enabled the team to recognize individual strengths and achieved a seemingly impossible task in less than a week**

- **Provide numbers as a means of quantification**

Numbers are a definitive measure of your performance. Backing up the previous point, numbers are a means of showing instead of telling to the employers what you have been up to and how well you have performed. The achievements appear to be rather vague if they are not properly quantified or described. The work experiences also need to be backed up by some numeric data in order to show your performance to the employer.

For instance, expressing in numerical terms how much growth the company experienced due to your efforts, or the increase in sales, or savings in budget or positive variances in performance is a clear indicator of your performance. Moreover, you can also express how big was your organization. It can help your prospective employer to have a sneak peek into your work experience.

- **Cut short all the unnecessary details**

One important element that the year tends to focus upon is brevity – concise, clear, relevant! Experts have been suggesting that too old an experience might not be considered relevant given the evolving trends. Even though you might be experienced in the same field, you need to focus on relevant and recent jobs accomplished. The rule is to have a resume that is only 1-2 pages long. Adding old experience will only lead to making your resume too lengthy, decreasing your chances of getting selected. Moreover, note that resume for each job application needs to be altered. This is because not all of the skills will be seen as relevant. A solution is to create an overlap of skills, abilities and knowledge.

One way to cover up your experience gap is to use a combination style resume. This way you can conceal the working gap while retaining a focus on relevant experience.

Another important suggestion is to go through the job description keenly and develop a resume hence wise. This way you will know whether you have the desired abilities and how can you present the best to your prospective employer. Do not panic if you do not have some of the mentioned skills – they can be easily acquired through training!

- **Using call-out boxes and breakaway text is the essence of resume**

Things appealing to the eye are usually easier to remember. A resume that engages the reader through visuals maintains interest and provides information that draw the reader's attention. Call-out boxes and breakaway text grab the attention and thus, appear to be most important part of the resume.

This can be proved by the fact that when reading anything, a magazine or a book, you tend to look at what is different – the boxes or the different styled font. Using this for your advantage, you can captivate the reader's mind by putting in a statement that can do nothing but get you selected.

> **The perfect visionary to make your organization *grow* and *stand out***

- **Deliver value by creating a value proposition – your highest selling bid!**

Your resume needs to deliver value to your prospective employer. This will entail that what is it that makes you stand out others and why they should be interviewing you. It pertains to be the most convincing reason for hiring you and as to why you should be given preference over others. This should include the actual 'value' you can deliver that no one else can and thus, pertains to be your highest selling bid. Use this opportunity and fill it up in your resume.

> **Able to implement SAP within one month**

- **Create a visually engaging resume**

You need to remember what catches your attention in a magazine. It is the graphics, the layout and the colors. Though your resume is not supposed to be a magazine, but it does need to contain some element that makes it appear appealing and attractive.

By using graphics, colors, attractive layout formats, graphs, charts, shadings, call-out boxes and breakaway text, borders and the list goes on, the attention for the reader can be grabbed, and for good. The reader is engaged with the attractiveness portrayed and you have made your first impression on your employer!

- **Customize your resume**

There is no rule as regards what constitutes a good resume and what needs to be included in it. Different employers look for different elements in it and each hold a differing opinion as regards what should be there. This may appear haunting to you, but you can also respond to this task by customizing your resume.

Customizing resume means altering it for specific requirements. This will enable the employers to see that they want. You also need to recognize the fact that how you position yourself is different from how the employers see you. Customizing your resume to the needs of the job in question can make the task of selection easier. You can pin point how you can add to the company's benefit and how can you respond to the needs of the company.

Do not forget to add plausible references. This will increase your chances of getting selected and add credibility to what you have written in your resume.

- **An impressive branding statement**

Your brand statement needs to be a part of your personal branding document, and needs to be highly impressive.

> **BUSINESS STRATEGIST with five years of experience developing the organizational, functional and business strategies, maintaining connections with different levels within the organization, seizing and coordinating growth opportunities, and creating a dynamic environment for growth**

- **Include a cover letter**

Inclusion of a cover letter as part of the job application is as important as the resume itself. A good cover letter might be the difference in getting the employer to read the resume or to move to the next application. Each job needs to have a different cover letter which means that as the resume needs to be customized, so does the cover letter. It must be in accordance with the specific position being applied for.

Do not use form letters like

> **This position in your company**

The letter needs to mention the specific job being applied for and also, the name of the company being applied to. Make sure there are no grammatical errors and that the cover letter is in a professional format. It should be neatly and watchfully crafted as the cover letter is what ensures that your resume will be read!

- **An Internet Profile**

With the availability of online information and the job postings available online, employers often tend to look for prospective employees through online forums. Building your portfolio on LinkedIn will help you entail greater advantages. The site also provides you with the option to add links that allow you to demonstrate your skills to the employers in a better manner.

Remember that your original resume will provide the basis for your LinkedIn profile and this profile can immensely increase your credibility in the eyes of the employers. This also opens the window of opportunity, with many people being head hunted through LinkedIn. Treat your LinkedIn profile like the gold that it is. You never know who will see it!

- **Diversity is the key!**

As the job market gets stronger, employers are more focused on finding employees with the right experience. This relates to diversity and the pivot has now shifted towards having diverse skills on board. Employers want you to be able to take responsibility, along with taking initiatives and sticking up to the best practices.

- **Reminder!**

It is important to remember that there is no one-size-fits-all resume. This concept has taken its roots from targeted positioning. Each resume needs to be created in correlation with the job requirements and industry to which you are applying. It should evolve with you and must be kept away from any sort of outdated, meaningless and repetitive information.

Utilize Personal Branding to your Benefit

The recruiters need to know your unique capabilities in an energetic flow that must tend to focus on the fact how you can enable the prospective company to save or generate money. As described before, personal branding is all about the benefits and values you can bring to a company. In order to make a strong impact with a lasting impression, it is a must have that all the necessary elements are put together in a qualitative and presentable manner. The key again is to have a document that leaves a lasting impression.

Experts have suggested that a great personal branding document has word of mouth potential. Therefore, you can use some of the questions to create your resume that will leave a deep impact.

- What is it that you love to do when at work?
- What problems are you capable of solving and how you intend to do it?
- How can you relate the work to daily life in order to enable your coworkers understand it better?
- Do you actually have proof for validating all of your propositions? What is it and how it can be presented?
- Entailing the skill, how you intend to utilize it for the greater benefit of the organization?

Answering these and some other similar questions will enable you to conclude some statements regarding yourself, which can have an impact on your potential career. Try to make statements that connect them all in light of your expertise.

Instead of using the job title in your resume to connect with your abilities, play with your branding statement and use it. You will experience that using a personal branding statement leaves a much deeper impact on the reader rather than the title. Let's consider this. If you write on your resume:

> **I am a counselor**

...your allowing others to judge you, form an opinion based on their own without understanding the profession, the value and the role. You will be put into a pool of people as opposed to standing out on your own merit. Instead, when you write

> **I love to help people develop their inner capabilities and help them get rid of unnecessary stress and demotivation. I use my own methodology of relieving the negative energies, providing a burst of positive energies as a means of building them up. Focusing on training, I customize the broader concepts according to each individual so they can make the company perform better**

... you are listing what it is exactly that you bring to the table. You are taking yourself out of a generic pool of professionals and your informing your future employer what specific value you will bring to their business. Note that your branding statement will be adjusted as needed, but the overall theme would remain the same. Through your branding statement, you want your employer to know what you do and how well you do it.

And this is the thing, which will get you going!

What not to do!

Remember that the traditional ways of writing up a resume are outdated now, and there is literally no space for them! There is a vivid difference in a resume that belongs to 2015 and in that which belongs to some other prior year.

- **Do not forget to add your personal profile!**

Personal profile is what is the prime focus this year. It should portray your abilities in relation to the job being applied for. When you have customized your profile in accordance with the desired job description, there is a high probability of you getting selected.

- **Do not get it too long to increase the length**

Create resumes that are short, to the point and clear. Lacking to do so will make you count amongst the rejected candidates.

- **Avoid listing skills in one place**

The skills should be properly arranged and put in an attractive section. It is primarily your skills that are getting you to the job.

- **Do not intermingle information**

Present information in a clear, presentable and arranged manner. Information must not be confusing to read, or the reader will lose interest and discontinue reading.

- **Do not focus on adding text**

Provide meaningful information – do not just add words to increase the length. This will lead to repetitive information, which is a must to avoid!

- **Do not make a general resume for all jobs**

Customization is a must! Gone are the days when a single resume was acceptable for all jobs. Now, a customized and a very relevant resume is required in order to hook to a good job.

A Sample!

Below, you will find sample of a cover letter and a resume that have been drafted for your guidance and set in line with the latest standards. These will help you design your own resume for future job applications. You may beef and tweak it to suit your personal needs although it is highly recommended that use the format as is so that you grab the utmost attention of your prospective employers. Not only this will help you present yourself amicably but will also lend you a good job which perfectly matches your skills and allows you to build yourself a bright and prosperous career using just one articulately devised smart document. So follow the advice given and let yourself grow!

Cover Letter for the Position of Financial Management Analyst

Dear Concerned

This letter is to introduce myself for the position of **Financial Management Analyst** for **XYZ**. My diversified and in-depth professional work experience at **ABC Company** coupled with a record of outstanding performance at both professional and academic level has enabled me to present myself as a potential candidate for a suitable position in your organization.

With an outstanding academic background and unique working exposure, I have been consistently providing my professional services that prove my determination and demonstrate my unyielding commitment to hard work for the accomplishment of my goals. I offer a good blend of professional experience, requisite knowledge and skills to become a vital member of your organization.

Being a Finance and International Business double major graduate from the Curtin University, I seek to further enhance my financial and management analytical skills to become a full-time business analyst.

My experience of using SAP SE has enabled me to sharpen my skills of business planning and analysis. Working as an **Accountant Intern** at **ABC Company** has allowed me to provide meaningful insights to portfolio managers. Other tasks included expediting analysis of incoming and outgoing payments. My analysis and valuation is based on financial models built using Microsoft Excel. The valuation techniques I have used so far are cash flow methodologies (free cash flows to firm and free cash flows to equity holders), price multiples approach (P/E multiples) and sum-of-parts valuation. I have successfully executed MIRO under supervised accounts payable and cash disbursement for proper recording of costs, compliance with cash disbursement process and allocation of high month-average expenses. In the area of accounts receivable collection, I have cooperated with teams to enable accurate recording of sales and billing execution process. This post has groomed me professionally and helped me further polish my analytical skills by broadening my exposure to various sectors.

I am looking for a career opportunity that is commensurate with my skills and qualification and that can provide me with a competitive working environment coupled with the opportunity for career growth. I look forward to hearing from you.

Regards,

Neil D. Walker

NEIL D. WALKER

Address	Residence		
Telephone ☎	Mobile	+1 (111) 111-111	
Email	Personal	neildwalker@gmail.com	

EDUCATION

Particulars		Session	
Bachelor of Science in Finance & International Business	Curtin University, Australia	May 2014	GPA 3.5
Associate's Degree, Business	King's Own Institute, Australia	May 2011	GPA 3.83
Relevant Coursework	Business Statistics, International Business, International Finance, Equity Analysis, Global Marketing		

OBJECTIVE

To obtain an exigent position in business world while at the same time advancing my professional knowledge, skills and experience and become part of a challenging and rapidly changing environment so that I can further sharpen my abilities.

EXPERIENCE

- **ABC Company. (Sydney)**
  Accountant Intern (Jan'12 to May'14)

  - Completion and fulfillment of the assigned administrative and accounting related responsibilities for the Eastern Regional Office
  - Successful and efficient administration of A/R(FBL5N) collection, A/P(FBL1N), and disbursement of cash (F-52) utilizing SAP SE
  - Formulation of management reports including weekly cash flow report and monthly forecasts by application of SAP SE and MS Excel
  - Operation of MIRP for the recording of accurate costs and formulation of outgoing payment on SAP SE

- **Hotel Paradise (Perth)**
  Front Desk Intern (Jun'12 to Aug'12)

  - Successful designing and implementation of a relevant database for accumulating information of 700 rooms
  - Used of Fidelio System on a routine basis
  - Rendering of quality customer services from around the world including interpretations to guests
  - Accommodation of VIP customers' needs and tabulation of their requests for future reference

- **Lee & Paik CPA (Melbourne)**
  Accountant Assistant (Jan'10 to Jun'10)

  - Management and recording of bank statements and other financial statements in QuickBooks Pro
  - Coordination with other accountants and accountant assistants to complete the assigned tasks
  - Effective communication with clients based on their reports and interests and accurate delivering to the supervisors
  - Team management and team work with other assistants to administer over 300 client's contract information

LEADERSHIP EXPERIENCE AND ACTIVITIES

- **Curtin University**
  Co-President (Jan'12 to May'14)

  - Administration, communication and implementation of the organization's vision, mission and overall direction
  - Arrangement of general meetings and events which raised the number of members (34 to 73)
  - Greatly fostered participation in activities
  - Drafting of financial planning including formulation of annual budget and monitoring its execution

- **XYZ Honor Society**
  Member (Feb'10 to May'13)

- **King's Own Institute Business & Economics Club**
  Member (Feb'10 to Sep'12)

  - Participation in diverse events such as stock stimulation, game contest and company visiting

IT PROFICIENCY

- Proficient in MS Office® applications (Word, Excel, Power Point, Publisher, Access)
- Proficient in using Oracle, SAP SE, Bloomberg Terminal and Fidelio System

HOBBIES AND INTERESTS

- Reading
- Sports

ACHIEVEMENTS

- Grew up the size of an organization named Korean Economics & Business Association

PERSONAL

- Marital status   :   Single
- Date of Birth   :
- Nationality   :   Australian
- Languages   :   English, French

REFERENCES

Will be furnished upon request

You have now come so far in your Resume Writing journey! If you feel confident in your abilities to write an outstanding resume then you can close this book right now. But if you want to take your resume to the next level than, please, continue reading! You will not be disappointed!

HOW TO WRITE AN OUTSTANDING RESUME

INTRODUCTION

Employers are forever on the lookout for the resume that jumps out at them. Not in terms of being fancy and pretty to look at. Employers are looking to be impressed! Reading your resume, they want to be able to feel that YOU are the right candidate for the job. They want to be able to do this before ever setting eyes on you!

Tall order, right? You betcha it is!

The very first step in landing that ideal job is to write an ideal resume and cover letter. Without those two most primary of introductions, there most likely won't be a first interview!

Taking That First Important Step

Your resume places you in the front lines when job hunting. It becomes your calling card. It is not about compelling drama or clever prose; it's a few simple pages, expertly written, containing information that is all about you.

Your resume will either place you front and center where all the good jobs are or it will not -- there is no middle ground.

It's Now or Never

With this lesson guide, your resume writing skills will become well honed and your resume will be fine tuned. You will learn to sell yourself with simple, yet, effective words. Your resume will not be relegated to the bottom of any pile -- it will be placed where it belongs....at the very top!

You will write a resume that will rival any resume written by a top-notch professional writer, and you will do this in complete confidence.

Let's Get Started!

EFFECTIVE RESUME AND COVER LETTER WRITING

To begin, make a decision to discard any former knowledge learned about the "rules" of resume and cover letter writing. People commonly become stuck in "bad" writing habits from a time gone by.

It is almost a certainty that since you last wrote your resume, much has been learned and even more has been changed. This is as it should be, for everyday, very creative people are adding to the resume and cover letter writing arsenal.

This guide is chock full of the most recent and cutting-edge resume and cover letter writing techniques, culled from writing professionals and employment experts.

The Basics

For years, we have been told that to be most effective, a resume should be only one page. This just does not apply any longer! Today's resume is creative and unique.

Aside from the most essential and key elements, a resume should reflect the personality and need of the job seeker and not be some cookie cutter rendition of what is "acceptable and expected."

Standards in resumes and cover letters have changed dramatically, but, only so far as the job seeker has the creative expression and know-how to pull it off! Therein lies the difference. Everyday, employers read all of the standard resumes. They are required to go through each and every one! But, which one will catch their eye?

Formatting in resumes and cover letters has expanded, too. When you consider that your resume will be your own, personalized form of marketing yourself -- this lends itself to all manner of unique communication and expression.

Again, so long as the essential elements are included in each resume and cover letter, you are at complete liberty to make certain that your resume will impress and with a bang!

Just how, exactly, does one do this?

First of all, learn about the most basic principles involved in writing a highly effective resume and cover letter. Once you have this down, the creative expression can begin!

Your most basic purpose in writing your resume and cover letter will be to be noticed among the many. You want to stand out as not just a good candidate but as "the" candidate just fitting for the job you want.

When you consider that next to your well written resume, not even one hundred other resumes will be written as well as yours, you can see the odds will be in your favor. Your salvation here is in writing a resume that will compel a perspective employer to notice your credentials. If you can master this technique, the rest will be pure gravy.

THE PURPOSE OF YOUR RESUME

Your resume is an important tool that communicates all about YOU. When it does the job right, you win an interview.

Your resume doesn't simply provide a prospective employer with your work history. It speaks loud and clear that you have the credentials needed to be a complete success in this new position or career.

Your resume will attract immediate attention. The reader will want to pick it up and read it top to bottom. Interest will be stimulated. An interview will be arranged.

Your resume will contain:

- ✓ Your contact information, i.e. name, address, phone, email address, website address.

- ✓ A defined job objective.

- ✓ A work history.

- ✓ Educational history.

- ✓ Affiliations.

- ✓ References.

Your resume will be written using professional grade printing and paper.

RESUME PRESENTATION IS KEY

An employer can have hundreds of boring resumes to pour through. This means when something catches the eye, it must really pop out!

Your resume must impress within the first important seconds or it will not impress at all. Employers will quickly scan all resumes and then grab for those that catch their eye best.

To write a really effective resume, you will use powerful statements that will impress. This is very important, but, you do not want to oversell! There is a very fine line here and you will learn all about it.

Above all, you will make honest statements about yourself. They will be strong statements and 100% true, or they will not be effective at all.

Just as you would sell any product that you believe strongly in, you will learn to sell the product that is you! Once you have learned to do this, you will find that you will get a better response from a prospective employer than other prospects do and even those with better credentials. It is all in how you market your product!

WOW THE EMPLOYER

First of all, who are you writing this resume for? Your prospective employer will be the one who oversees the day to day operations of the company you want to join.

They make the hiring decisions and they are entirely invested in ensuring that you are the right one for the job. This person will care about whether or not you can do a good job for that company and so this is the one you are writing your resume for.

You want to be sure that you are the right candidate for the job. You want to be sure you know everything there is to know about this company. You want to understand exactly, which qualities are needed to be the right candidate for this job.

You want to be sure you are not a good candidate for this job, but, that you are the best candidate for this job.

Time to start writing

This is the time to put pen to paper and to lay out clearly what your prospective employer is looking for in an ideal candidate. You need to be able to solidify what it is that you bring to the table, even before you begin.

Jot down every fine point about your training and experience, your unique characteristics, special talents, even your attitude -- everything that shows you most qualified for the job you seek.

If you are new to the job market, be creative and draw on your upbringing, life exposure and anything that can account for your unique experience and qualities.

You will begin to be able to connect the dots during this process. Simple statements will turn into sentences and sentences into paragraphs. Keep this information in a safe place. You will use it later to be incorporated into your finished product.

ELEMENTS OF A RESUME THAT WILL IMPRESS

The primary element of an ideal resume contains powerful and assertive statements about your talents, characteristics and accomplishments. No need to be shy. You are going for the gold so sell yourself with all that is in you!

The secondary element of an ideal resume will show "you know your stuff" and know it well! This will be proven by education, experience, work history and any other relevant affiliations that shows the prospective employer that you are a person of substance and not only of design.

Keep in mind that the more standard resume will simply be a chronological account of a very boring life and most people will not give it a second glance. Write your resume to be interesting and even impressive and watch as your phone rings for that important interview!

You will write a resume that does much more than just inform; you will write a resume that compels to action! Your resume will become as a good bargaining tool! Your prospective employer will be interested and will stand up and take notice! This is exactly what you want.

Be bold about your assertive statements, but, not too bold. Leave them wanting for more. Tease a bit with nuggets of information and let them be interested to know more.

WRITING YOUR OBJECTIVE

Be very clear in defining the name of the job or job title you are so qualified for. Be specific. Avoid general terms such as: I am seeking a Management position. Well, OK, but what kind of Management position are you seeking? Marketers signal in on one product at a time and so will you!

You will hit the bull's eye when you define your precise career direction and put that down on paper. When your prospective employer reads it, they should have no doubt that you are seeking the exact job that they need filled.

After starting your resume with your contact information, your next section will clearly start with your job objective. Once your prospective employer can see that what you bring to the table is what they want, they will continue to scan for more.

Employers separate the wheat from the chaff very quickly. They look for objectives that meet with their own expectations. They know there are many prospects out there that really don't know what they want.

Employers are not looking for these types. Your objective will convey that your objective proves you will make the kind of contributions to the company that they need and want.

Keep in mind, too, that an employer is looking for a candidate who will meet their own needs, and not for one who is looking to meet his or her own goals and agenda.

Your goal can be to offer this company your unique skill set and experience, but, the key is in putting that across in a way that proves you are their to service them and not the other way around.

Your resume must grab them within the first few seconds, so, your objective must be dynamite! Clearly state the job title you are going for and then add a few key phrases to show you will meet their exact needs...more on this later.

WRITING YOUR SUMMARY

The Summary element of your resume needs to pack a punch to be most effective. It contains the best about how and why you qualify for the job.

You want the employer to focus in quickly on this section because it will highlight your most important accomplishments, talents, and qualities.

After reading your Summary, the employer should know, without any doubt, that you are the best man or woman for the job. This is where you will shine! This will be your moment to show your stuff. After reading this section, the employer will be compelled to read more!

Writing this section, you will use many colorful and descriptive words. If one of your best talents is sales, write that you are a gifted salesman, able to close the deal in record time!

If your talent is hairdressing, write that your creations have been featured at XYZ hair show and that your technique is now copied in Salons throughout the Mid-West! You get the idea.

This section will only contain information about you that is commendable and that will set you apart from the crowd. Using the right kind of descriptive, complimentary words, you achieve this handsomely. Your summary will show your prospective employer that you alone will be the best fit for the position needed to be filled.

Tailor your Summary to your Prospective Employer's Needs

Before writing your resume, you wrote notes on what makes you the best candidate for your intended position. You will have looked at the many characteristics and qualities that you believe your prospective employer will be looking for in the ideal candidate.

Now is the time to tailor your Summary section to matching those specific needs. Every statement made in your Summary section will be targeted to show the employer that you have what it takes to fill that position.

Work on writing positive and affirming statements that exemplify your unique abilities and talents to be most affective in the intended position. Practice using descriptive words.

If you want to write that you are a good leader, write instead that you are "proven leader" with initiative and motivational skills that cause others to act! Describe why you are good at what you do and leave no room for interpretation.

Using words like "good" and "competent" speaks in general terms. Describe how you possess these attributes and you will have done your job well!

Below, you will find a variety of suggestions for composing your Summary section. You can select those that best suit your skill-set. Experiment a bit, first, and then zero in on those that best reflect what you have to offer a perspective employer. Remember, your Summary section is critical to your resumes success.

Few people will use all of the suggestions. Doing this might be seen as over-kill. You are encouraged to say the most, while writing the least.

- ✓ Start with a concise phrase that describes your profession.
- ✓ Next, another concise phrase showing your broad or specialized experience.
- ✓ Make a few more concise statements to show the following:
    - the full extent of your skill-set
    - the variety of your skills
    - diversity in your experience
    - an accomplishment worth noting
    - Anything remarkable about your accomplishments.

Optional

- ✓ Professional achievements
- ✓ Personal Characteristics worth noting
- ✓ Concise statement to highlight professional objective.

WRITING THE SKILLS AND ACCOMPLISHMENTS SECTION

In the Summary section of your resume, you can brag a little. In the Skills and Accomplishments section you can brag a little more.

This section will cap off all that qualifies you for your intended position. You will show your prospective employer that there can be no other and the journey stops with YOU!

How do you do this best? You continue to show that you are the right one for the job by going into better detail about all that you wrote of in your Summary section. This requires careful wording so as not to be repetitious. If you can pull this off professionally, using words that glow, you will have the attention you are looking for!

The most key point about writing this section is you are not going to inform. You are going to highlight in more detail, what your prospective employer already believes to be true about you as an ideal candidate.

The Purpose of your Skills and Accomplishments Section

Go into good detail about the following:

- Any benchmarks or landmarks accomplished as the result of your unique skill-set.

- Using facts, figures and statistics, show how your best efforts showed the best results.

- Your specific talents and unique gifts as related to your job.

- All accomplishments that sets you apart.

To be most effective, you will use clear, crisp writing that sums up. You are going into detail here, but not so much that this section reads like a story.

Key Point -- Write so that you give hints and not complete details. You want your prospective employer to call you in for the interview to learn more! This is critical.

CONGRATULATIONS ON TAKING ACTION TO ENSURE YOU LAND YOUR DREAM JOB

www.ingramcontent.com/pod-product-compliance
Lightning Source LLC
Chambersburg PA
CBHW070801180526
45168CB00004B/1706